POLAR ANIMALS

mibo®

Button
BOOKS

MADELEINE ROGERS

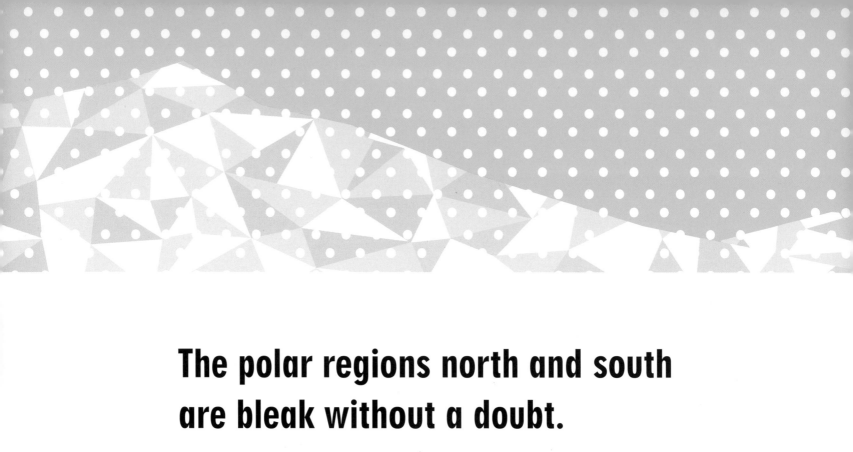

The polar regions north and south
are bleak without a doubt.

But look again; you're sure to see some animals about.

Penguins do not fly but swim.
Their wings go flip and flop.

They lay an egg upon the ice
and then they sit on top.

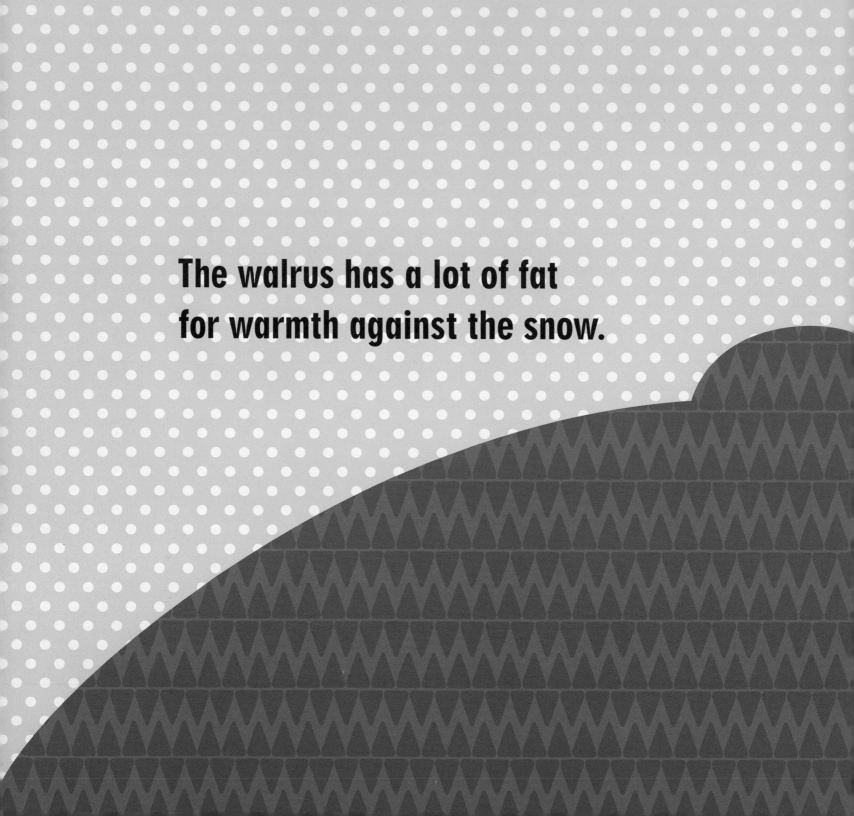

The walrus has a lot of fat
for warmth against the snow.

His massive tusks can break the ice
in case he's stuck below.

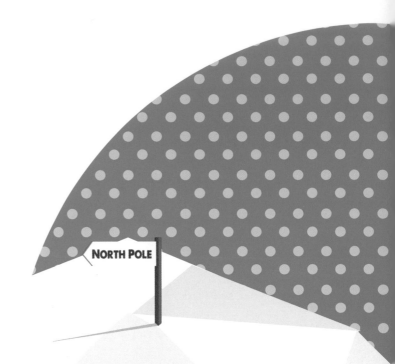

NORTH POLE

You might just spot a polar bear
not far from the North Pole.

She has her babies underground in a cozy little hole.

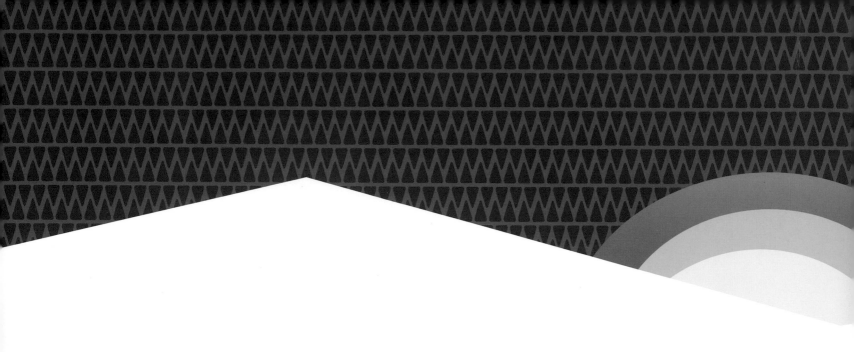

Reindeer are good at smelling food
deep beneath the ice.

They dig with their enormous hooves

till they taste something nice.

Snowy owls are born dark gray, becoming white as they get older.

They make their feathered nests
atop a sturdy rock or boulder.

These polar parts are freezing cold.
For now, at least, that's true.
Our frosty friends just love it here.
They're wondering: would you?